New York in the American Revolution

Daniel R. Faust

PowerKiDS press™

New York

Published in 2015 by The Rosen Publishing Group, Inc.
29 East 21st Street, New York, NY 10010

Book Design: Chris Brand

Photo Credits: Cover, MPI/Archive Photos/Getty Images; p. 5 Universal Images Group/ Contributor/Getty Images; p. 7 U.S. National Archives; pp. 7, 9, 13 (inset) © Corbis; p. 11 © Lee Snider/Corbis; p. 11 (inset) Courtesy U.S. Naval Historical Center; p. 13 © NorthWind Picture Archives; p. 15 Interim Archives/Contributor/Archive Photos/ Getty Images; p. 15 (inset) The New York Public Library/Art Resource; p. 17 Printed with permission of the Utica Public Library, Utica, New York; p. 19 De Agostini/Getty Images; p. 21 Library of Congress Prints and Photographs Division, Washington, DC.

Library of Congress Cataloging-in-Publication Data

Faust, Daniel R.
New York in the American Revolution / by Daniel R. Faust.
p. cm. — (Spotlight on New York)
Includes index.
ISBN 978-1-4777-7332-1 (pbk.)
ISBN 978-1-4777-6389-6 (6-pack)
ISBN 978-1-4777-7329-1 (library binding)
1. New York (N.Y.)—History—Revolution, 1775-1783—Juvenile literature. 2. New York (N.Y.)— History—Juvenile literature. I. Faust, Daniel R. II. Title.
E230.5.N4 F38 2015
974.7—d23

Manufactured in the United States of America

CPSIA Compliance Information: Batch #WS15RC: For further information contact Rosen Publishing, New York, New York at 1-800-237-9932.

Contents

English Colonies in America

After their victory over the French in the **French and Indian War**, the British controlled most of North America east of the Mississippi River, from Nova Scotia in modern-day Canada to Florida and the Caribbean. The British spent a lot of money in their war with the French and needed even more money to repay the war **debt** and run the new **colonies** they had taken after the war.

The British **Parliament** passed laws that made the people living in their American colonies pay new taxes. The Sugar Act of 1764 required colonists to pay a tax on foreign products like sugar, wine, and coffee, and limited the export of lumber, iron, and other products from the colonies to other countries. The Currency Act of 1764 made the paper money that was printed and used in the colonies illegal. In 1765, Parliament passed the Stamp Act. It forced the American colonists to use special paper for all printed materials, like newspapers, legal documents, and even playing cards. The Stamp Act was named after the tax stamp that was attached to each piece of this paper. Many colonists thought these laws were unfair because colonists did not elect people to Parliament.

The British Parliament is composed of two houses, the House of Lords and the House of Commons. Membership in the House of Lords is inherited, while members of the House of Commons are elected. This engraving depicts the House of Commons in the late eighteenth century.

The Stamp Act Congress Meets in New York City

While some colonists **protested** the Stamp Act with violence, others decided to use a more peaceful approach. In October 1765, the Stamp Act Congress met in New York City. Nine of the **Thirteen Colonies** sent **delegates** to the meeting. There were 27 delegates in all.

Working together, the members of the Stamp Act Congress wrote the Declaration of Rights and **Grievances**. This declaration listed fourteen points of protest among the colonists, including the belief that the colonists should have the same rights as the people in Great Britain and the belief that Parliament could not tax the colonists without their consent.

Some of the delegates refused to sign the Declaration of Rights and Grievances. They believed it did not go far enough to protect the rights of the colonists. Even though it was not signed by all 27 delegates, the declaration was sent to the British Parliament, which rejected it.

The Stamp Act taxed all printed goods and legal papers. Stamps, like the ones shown here, were placed on the papers to show that a tax had been paid on them. Also shown is a political cartoon from a colonial newspaper, which is a good example of the colonists' unhappiness with these taxes.

A political cartoon from a newspaper

Choosing Sides

Some colonists rejected Great Britain's control over the colonies. These people were called **patriots**. They felt that the British government had too much power and taxed them unfairly. Colonists who supported British control and remained **loyal** to Great Britain were called loyalists. New York had more loyalists than any other colony.

The Sons of Liberty was a group of patriots that formed in Boston, Massachusetts. Soon, Sons of Liberty chapters formed in the other colonies. In New York, the Sons of Liberty clashed with the British authorities over liberty "trees," tall wooden poles that were raised to protest unpopular British laws. In January 1770, a group of patriots in New York City fought with a group of British soldiers who were trying to cut down a liberty tree. This event became known as the Battle of Golden Hill and is considered to be the first conflict between colonists and British troops.

In 1775, patriots formed the New York Provisional Congress as a replacement for the loyalist New York Assembly. The Sons of Liberty formed a **militia** and forced William Tryon, the British governor, to take **refuge** on a British warship in New York Harbor.

In the years leading up to and during the war, colonists often publicly protested against British control. During one protest in New York City, angry colonists even pulled down a statue of King George III! The statue was melted down to make bullets to use in the war.

Taking Fort Ticonderoga

Fort Ticonderoga, located in northern New York at the southern end of Lake Champlain, was controlled by British forces. Fighting there helped the British defeat the French during the French and Indian War. The lake's northern tip reaches into Canada, which the British also controlled. This made it easy for the British to bring supplies and troops down from Canada into the colonies.

Ethan Allen was a patriot who led a group of **civilian** soldiers called the Green Mountain Boys. They lived in what is now Vermont, an area claimed by New York State. The Green Mountain Boys did not want to be ruled by either New York or Great Britain. On May 10, 1775, they attacked Fort Ticonderoga. The British, with less than fifty men inside the fort, were not ready for the attack. Allen and his men took control of the fort without firing a single shot. The patriots did not have many cannons, and the weapons that Allen's men captured at Ticonderoga helped the **Continental army** fight the American Revolution.

Allen is still remembered as a hero in northern New York and Vermont. Another soldier who helped capture Fort Ticonderoga, Benedict Arnold, later became a **traitor** to the patriot cause.

Ethan Allen

IN THE ... HOVAH
AND TH... CONGRESS
ETHAN ALLE... 1737~1789

After Ethan Allen and the Green Mountain Boys took control of Fort Ticonderoga, there were frequent battles with the British for control of the fort. The British took the fort back in 1777, then burned the buildings and abandoned the fort. The larger picture shows Fort Ticonderoga as it looks today.

The Battle of Long Island

In April 1776, General George Washington, commander of the Continental army, moved the patriot forces from Boston, Massachusetts, to Manhattan. He knew that the British wanted to attack New York City. Whoever controlled the major port at New York City would also control the Hudson River and the Mohawk Valley, which provided access to the interior of North America. British control of New York would also separate the northern colonies from the southern colonies.

In July, the British sent a **fleet** of 500 ships and 35,000 soldiers to New York Harbor. Under the command of General William Howe, the British forces gathered on Staten Island. In August, Washington sent troops across the East River from Manhattan Island to defend Brooklyn Heights on Long Island. The British forces attacked the Continental army there. The patriots were split up and outnumbered. The Continental army was defeated. After the Battle of Long Island, Washington and his troops snuck across the East River to Manhattan during the foggy night of August 29, 1776. The patriot army **retreated**, eventually crossing from New York into New Jersey.

General William Howe

This painting shows patriot soldiers fighting at the Battle of Long Island. After Washington's army was beaten there, they were forced to retreat north. The small picture shows General William Howe, who was named commander in chief of Great Britain's army in October 1775.

The British Take New York City

After the patriot army retreated, the British took full control of New York City, Long Island, and southeastern New York. New York City became the headquarters of the British army. It stayed under British control until the end of the American Revolution. Patriot soldiers built forts along the Hudson River to keep the British in New York City. To keep the British navy from sailing up the Hudson River, the patriots placed a 500-yard chain across the river between West Point and Constitution Island. The **links** of this "Great Chain" were two feet in length and weighed 114 pounds.

During the Battle of Long Island, General Washington had sent Nathan Hale behind enemy lines to spy on the British troops. Shortly after the British took control, the Great Fire of 1776 destroyed about a third of New York City. The British arrested many **suspected** patriots, including Nathan Hale. On September 22, Hale was hanged. Unlike Hale, most patriots captured or arrested by the British were simply sent to jail. When the jails became too crowded, the British started using **abandoned** warships in New York Harbor as floating jails. One of these prisons ships was the HMS *Jersey*. Thousands of men died on the *Jersey* as a result of disease, **starvation**, and torture.

This illustration, made in the late nineteenth century, depicts Nathan Hale's execution by the British. Hale is shown giving his supposed last words, "I only regret that I have but one life to give for my country." The smaller image shows the HMS *Jersey*, one of the ships used by the British as floating prisons during the American Revolution.

Native American Enemies and Allies

The American Revolution divided the tribes of the Six Nations. The Mohawks, Onondagas, Cayugas, and Senecas **allied** themselves with the British because of a history of trade and relations with the British. The Oneidas offered their services to the patriots. Some Tuscaroras fought with the patriots, while others sided with the British. Algonquian-speaking tribes like the Mahicans and Wappingers and other Munsees also fought with the patriots.

Joseph Brant, a Mohawk chief, and Sagoyewatha, a Seneca chief, both fought for the British. Sagoyewatha was also known as Red Jacket, after the coat that the British had given him. The Oneida chief Han Yerry assembled a group of Oneida warriors to serve as guides and scouts for patriot soldiers. Han Yerry, his wife Tyonajanegen, and their son Cornelius fought for the patriots at Oriskany, Saratoga, and Barren Hill.

The British and their Native American allies raided farms and villages on the **frontier** of New York and Pennsylvania. After the Cherry Valley Massacre in November 1778, Washington ordered his armies to attack and destroy every Iroquois and other Indian village they encountered in the New York region along with the crops in the Indians' fields.

The Battle of Oriskany was one of the few battles in the American Revolution in which British soldiers did not fight. Loyalists and their Native American allies fought the patriots, who were joined by members of the Oneida tribe, leading to internal conflict within the Iroquois Confederacy. This painting from 1901 shows patriot general Nicholas Herkimer, who was wounded in the battle and died soon after.

The British Stopped at Saratoga

The British hoped to split the New England colonies from the other colonies by capturing the Hudson River. British general John Burgoyne moved his troops south from Canada, recapturing Fort Ticonderoga in July 1777. Howe was supposed to move his troops north from New York City and Brigadier-General Barry St. Leger was supposed to move his troops east from western New York and Canada. General Nicholas Herkimer fought the British and their Mohawk and Seneca allies at Oriskany, saving Fort Stanwix in the Mohawk Valley and stopping St. Leger's invasion. Most of Herkimer's soldiers were **descendants** of German settlers or members of the Oneida tribe. Howe sent his troops to attack Philadelphia instead of up the Hudson River, leaving Burgoyne's men to fight the patriots alone.

On September 19, 1777, Burgoyne's men attacked American forces at Freeman's Farm, on the Hudson River near where Saratoga Springs is today. The British were outnumbered, but Burgoyne didn't retreat. On October 7, Burgoyne attacked again at Bemis Heights. Burgoyne's army **surrendered** 10 days later, a major victory for the patriots. These two conflicts were known as the Battles of Saratoga.

General Benedict Arnold's actions at the Battles of Saratoga made him a hero of the American Revolution. Arnold never received the rewards he felt he deserved, which was part of the reason he would later join the British side.

The End of the War

After Saratoga, fighting in New York slowed down except for frontier raids in the Mohawk Valley. Washington kept several thousand soldiers near Newburgh until the war's end. The last big battle of the American Revolution was fought in Yorktown, Virginia. In part because of the victory at Saratoga, the French had decided to help the patriots. During the summers of 1780 and 1781, French troops arrived in Virginia to help the colonists. Washington's troops and French forces surrounded the British leader, General Charles Cornwallis. The battle lasted nearly a month. Cornwallis surrendered on October 19, 1781. Fighting continued for two more years. Finally, in 1783, both sides signed the Treaty of Paris.

Despite Cornwallis's surrender, British forces continued to control New York until Evacuation Day on November 25, 1783. On December 4, 1783, Washington called his officers to Fraunces Tavern in New York City. He told them that he would **resign** from the army and return to civilian life.

This nineteenth-century print shows Washington entering New York City on Evacuation Day. Many of New York's loyalists left the city along with the British troops and resettled in Canada. The city's patriots greeted Washington with cheers. New Yorkers celebrated Evacuation Day every year until the early twentieth century.

New York's Revolutionary Leaders

During the American Revolution, New York's people played important roles. Thousands of New Yorkers helped fight for freedom. Some, such as Robert Livingston, became leaders. Livingston was one of New York's delegates to the First and Second Continental Congresses. Members of both congresses made important decisions about the new country. Livingston helped write the Declaration of Independence in 1776.

Educated as a lawyer, John Jay also served as a delegate to the First Continental Congress. In 1777, he helped write the New York State **constitution**, which created a new government for the state. Jay was chosen to be the first chief justice of the Supreme Court under the new United States Constitution in 1789.

Alexander Hamilton was another leader from New York. He fought in the revolution and was George Washington's **aide**. He helped write the United States Constitution. He was the country's first **secretary of the treasury**. He was a leader of one of the country's first **political parties**, the Federalist Party. It does not exist anymore but was very powerful at the time.

Glossary

abandoned: Left completely and finally.

aide: An assistant or helper.

allied: Joined by treaty, agreement, or common cause.

civilian: A person who is not on active duty with a military or law enforcement organization.

colonies: Regions settled by people from another land who keep their loyalty to their homeland.

constitution: The laws by which a country or state is governed.

Continental army: The American army during the American Revolution.

debt: Something that is owed, such as money, goods, or services.

delegates: People elected or chosen to act for or represent others.

descendants: People who are related to a person or group of people who lived in the past.

fleet: The largest organized unit of naval ships.

French and Indian War: The name given to that part of the Seven Years' War that was fought in North America between the French and their Native American allies and the British and their Native American allies.

frontier: The border between two different nations or cultures.

grievances: Complaints about practices that one believes to be wrong.

links: The rings or separate pieces that compose a chain.

loyal: Faithful to one's leader, government, or state.

militia: A group of citizens who are not soldiers but are trained and ready to fight when needed.

Parliament: The part of the British government, composed of the House of Lords and the House of Commons, that is responsible for making laws.

patriots: The colonists in the Thirteen Colonies who rebelled against British control during the American Revolution.

political parties: Groups of people organized to gain and exercise political power.

protested: Expressed objection to or disapproval of something.

refuge: A place that provides shelter or protection from danger.

resign: To formally give up an office, job, or position.

retreated: Moved away from an enemy in defeat or to seek a more beneficial position.

secretary of the treasury: The person in charge of a government's economic and financial policies.

starvation: Suffering or death caused by hunger.

surrendered: Gave up possession of something to another.

suspected: Believed to be guilty.

Thirteen Colonies: The thirteen British colonies along the mid-Atlantic coast of North America, which would join together and fight for their independence from Britain and become the United States of America.

traitor: A person who betrays a country or group of people by helping or supporting the enemy.

Index

Primary Source List

Page 7 (inset). *This is the place to affix the stamp.* Published by Pennsylvania Journal and Weekly Advertiser. 1765. Now kept at the Library of Congress Prints and Photographs Division, Washington, DC.

Page 13 (inset). *The Honerable Sir William Howe. Knight of the Bath, & Commander in Chief of His Majesty's Forces in America.* Created by Richard Purcell, published by John Morris. Mezzotint print. 1777. Now kept at the Brown University Library, Providence, Rhode Island.

Websites

Due to the changing nature of Internet links, Rosen Publishing has developed an online list of websites related to the subject of this book. This site is updated regularly. Please use this link to access the list: **http://www.rcbmlinks.com/nysh/clrw**